Uncertain Behavior

Meredith Winn

Published by Folly Cove Publishing
visit www.meredithwinn.com

This book is a work of nonfiction, reflecting the author's
memories and perspective. While based on real events,
some details have been altered for privacy.

ISBN: 979-8-9986230-1-1
Printed in the United States of America

My words are for you.
For today, for yesterday, for always.
For the stories that follow us like shadows.
For the voices to share them, and the hearts that listen.
And for all that's left unspoken.

"I like a good story and I also like staring at the sea.
Do I have to choose between the two?"
- David Byrne

Prologue
August 2014

The sewing circle of my past floats like an illusion through clouded vision. We are generations of women: newlyweds, single mothers, immigrants and grandmothers, young and old. We sew our differences aside. The fabric of life twists and alters, ending in a display of fitted suits and custom wedding dresses.

This is how we work - women guiding women through transitions, customs and rituals. Pins and needles, full-length mirrors. Our needles move over, under and through.

We tell our stories through the hands of sewing. We find each other in vulnerability, and in doing so we learn of our own strength. For years I sat with piles of brokenness and found ways to repair it all. Darn, knit, mend. The sure-footedness of my youth carried me on wings of hope with the knowledge and belief that anything could be fixed. I am older now and life has grown exponentially in all directions. Anticipating my mother's imminent death reveals to me that some things cannot be fixed; life is best spent mending hearts.

My mother has not been my mother for five years now. Her progressive form of dementia ripped her abruptly from me, during the early years of mothering. This became the unraveling of a favorite sweater, caught on a nail, gone before I could say goodbye.

Her illness has consumed her. It defines her, and therefore defines me as well. She and I, we are a different sort of mother and daughter now. We are kindred spirits tied by an invisible string, meeting somewhere not in this world but in the air and space of sleep. We meet briefly in dreams before floating away from each other once again. Five years feels like forever, and peace comes slowly through the many faces of grief. At times I am stumbling and angry, weeping and broken, occasionally indifferent. Healing is marked by seasons: grief has an abrupt beginning and no clear end. Her unraveling mind helps me greet grace, because there's nothing left to do but find peace while I watch my mother slowly die.

Back before the diagnosis, before the emotional disconnect that resulted from a deteriorating frontal lobe, before her seizures and social awkwardness, before the endless lines of doctors that led us to the office of an unsmiling neurologist, before MRIs and EEGs and cognitive impairment tests, before adult diapers, walkers and wheelchairs, before Picks Disease - there was Mom.

When I was a young girl without sisters of my own, my mother's friendships taught me about the strength and resiliency of women. Thirty years later, her terminal illness teaches me even more about the human spirit. Life provides no answers. My mother has no sisters of her own either, so when news spread of the diagnosis, her lifelong friends circled around me to become my honorary aunties. I embraced the female power of her chosen collective and it continues to carry me, all these years later. It's through the stages of my mother's dementia that I see the peeling of life's layers and I accept the reality of how families cope with loss. I witness the friendships that remain and the love that rises.

When mothers forget how to mother, daughters are reluctant to step into their place. The early years of my Mom's terminal illness fractured us. This raw truth is now a memory attached to me in my own detachment. Her memory drifts like balloons tied to a child's wrist. That space between here and there is dappled in sunlight.

It is one part heavy, one part light.

Put a family in crisis and you'll discover coping mechanisms. They pop up like mushrooms after a rain. Laughter becomes medicine. Anger and bitterness flood the house. Tears become healing reserves of sanity. Put a family in crisis and you'll feel the floor shift and creak as everyone takes a step to the left, filling new shoes, bridging the gaps, taking on new roles. We are the brave ones; with swollen puffy eyes, we bear witness to each other. As we fade and reassemble (stubbornly at first) we provide each other space to grieve in our own strange ways. We are a different family now without Mom as matriarch.

In my heart there lays hidden a wail of melancholic verse sung with head thrown back. It's the stifled sob cried softly into deep pillows while the dark swallows me up from the outside in. Somewhere deep down there's an ache and a longing for something long lost. I simultaneously slide forward and backwards. Skating along the timeline that fluctuates between mother and daughter, adult and child.

What we do not know is the beginning. How and when she first sensed her mind had gone awry. What we do not know is the end. How and when the breath will leave her body and she will at once be free. All we know is here and now. Her humming, her vacant stares, her mouth agape filled with a void of words that will never cross her lips again.

Through the years of her illness, I have found beauty in the breakdown. There are surprising gifts. New relationships have the opportunity to bloom. Father and daughter heal, mend and make peace in her absence. Small talk grows bigger with the severity of our situation. Our conversations turn business-like without warning.

My father addresses health concerns, bills, receipts and the truth that she has outlived her long-term health insurance. He asks me a favor and I accept, knowing it will be near impossible for me to accomplish.

The truth is that I don't want to write my mother's obituary. I'm cursed with her superstitions. Perhaps I fear that when it's finished, her spirit will cut free from her body and she'll fly away from us for good. In my grieving mind, if I don't write her obituary, she can't die.

Strangely, nighttime has a cloak of comfort. The truth is that reality happens in the middle of the day. Three o'clock on a Tuesday afternoon. Yes, right now... the phone is ringing. I answer it expecting the worst, fearing that every call might be the one that brings me to my knees.

My mother is happily unaware and has not been lucid for years. She has required twenty-four hour nursing home care since 2010. My father became the caregiver during the first year of her illness, when she was still able to live at home. Now he lives alone with forty-eight years of marriage.

So, on the phone now - it's my father's voice in a panic that I hear. With one ear pressed to the phone I realize I am now a grown-up. He begins each conversation with "Your mother is fine." Because we both know that her death is always hovering in our minds. But his voice cracks, and there's a silent sob that hangs between us causing my eyes to well with tears. In this moment he is unsure, unsteady and unable to go it alone.

Through the years of my mother's decline, my father has become beautifully human to me. It's painful for men of his generation to reveal their humanness, brokenness or vulnerability. I'm thankful to be on the other end of his phone. I'm glad we have each other. After he clears his throat, he's asking questions and I'm providing the answers that I've grown to hate: we are in the final-stage of dementia and there's nothing pretty about it. The obsessive-compulsive behavior is behind us now. She is mute. There won't be any more anger or broken bones now, because she has declined so rapidly. Her wheelchair is permanent She will spend more and more of her time sleeping, and eventually her body will forget how to swallow. "Keep a list of emergency contacts in your wallet, Dad, and call me anytime you need."

I say things like, *When you're ninety-seven years old...* to remind him that he's going to get through this. "Dad, when you're ninety-seven, I'll be a sixty-year old woman. You'll still be tinkering with your lamps! I'll have to come over and find all the parts you misplaced." He laughs but he doesn't believe me, even though longevity runs in his family. I say things like this to remind us both that we will get through this, as unbelievable as it seems now. While walking so close to the edge of death, it's hard for him to think of being alone for another twenty years after my mom passes away.

So, we're left drifting, together yet separate. Bobbling in the hot sun as waves go up and down, making us queasy. There are no words other than sad and heart wrenching ones. Nothing left to share but sorrow and love.

I am wrapped in hand-sewn quilts for protection, for this is how I get through the winter of my grief. A sewing circle of past and present. I am surrounded not only by intricate patterns, personalities of creative women and the precision of their hand stitches, but I am embraced by their stories, the power of their words, the strength of memory and how they lived through healthier times.

These stories and quilts are what strengthen me with reminders that human imperfection is actually quite beautiful. In this life, we are all perfectly imperfect.

I pick up a needle and thread. I sew buttons, I patch jeans, I make tidy repairs for the things in my life that allow for mending. I cradle the phone on my shoulder and with a red thread between us, I speak to my mother's hospice nurse, 670 miles away. "Comfort and dignity," she tells me.

It's what the life of my beautiful mother has come to. I repeat it like a mantra, comfort and dignity; like a final goodbye that hangs in the distance.

My needle passes over, under and through.

Sewing my life with bits of her thread.

Until her story becomes my own.

Part I

Chapter One
June 2016

There are too many words. There are not enough words. There is acceptance like a wave; submission. And then there is strength, wisdom that arrives with time and compassion that feels like a bloodletting. There is confusion mixed with sadness and the bitterness that rises occasionally, it's all loosely stitched with threads of memory.

Why or how it's possible that my father recognizes me, but not his wife. His denial, his pain, his sleepy brain. And then there's his hospice nurse in baby blue scrubs to match my father's eyes. Her one sentence spoken aloud with a sudden realization of our situation; seeing me sandwiched between both parents, holding two sets of hands. Between writing notes and reading pulses, she whispers aloud to me,

"Bless your heart."

Six months ago my phone rang at lunch time on Christmas Eve, a hospital 670 miles away was looking for a daughter named Meredith Winn. "That's me." I say.

"I'm the daughter."

Every call from Virginia for the past seven years had always held the sad possibility of my mother's death. I held my breath, bracing myself against the silence coming from the other end of the line as a head nurse shuffled papers.

"Your father fell while Christmas shopping?"

It was a question, not a statement.

He was alone shopping for a wallet when his world came crashing down. A present for himself, no doubt, as he was prone to do over the years, driving my mother crazy when he'd come home with the exact thing he wanted.

He would never come home from this shopping trip. A sudden stroke, building on top of many small strokes over the years; and he fell to the tile floor, hitting his head. He remained there, unconscious. Someone called an ambulance, the manager, perhaps. And he lay there alone, bleeding on the department store floor until paramedics arrived. The collar and buttons of his blue polo shirt were covered in blood, an EMT cut it straight up the center with scissors.

The head nurse on the other end of the phone finishes her sentence, "It appears he's suffered a Traumatic Brain Injury and a fractured skull. He's here at the hospital in Intensive Care. Are you his power of attorney?"

It's Christmas Eve.

Fall on your knees, oh hear the angels voices.

2

Catching a flight on Christmas in a New England blizzard was next to impossible. I arrive on Boxing Day, and thus began six months of paperwork and long distance shuffling of flights from Maine to Virginia.

To see my Dad curled in fetal position, to see my Dad rip off his clothes and demand to be naked in the rehab center, to see my Dad with his head in his hands and a blank stare on his face, to see my Dad in pain, in sleep, in another reality all together.

Six months of tests and doctors appointments and anger (his) and sadness (mine) and overwhelm (ours). Six months of being the adult child caring for two incapacitated parents. Six months and we have landed on a strange planet where he resides now, with a Vascular Dementia diagnosis, living in the same nursing home as my mother, his wife of nearly fifty years. They are roommates, only she doesn't know it, because she is at end-of-life. They are roommates, only he doesn't know it, because he simply thinks he's visiting her as he's done for the past six years.

Life repeats now and I'm fascinated by how the brain, deep in dementia, functions to produce the reality it reveals like an old film reel flickering and jumping behind closed eyes. When my mother was first diagnosed with frontal lobe dementia many years ago, she told me the year was 1970. Her frustration and exhaustion from mothering two young toddlers is what connected us, back when I was thirty-four. It's been seven years? How is it possible that I am now forty-one and today my father says the year is 1969.

The director of the nursing home told me he woke this morning upset by the delusion that my mother had died. He demanded they find her body, as if she were not sleeping in the hospital bed five feet from his. I shake the visual from my mind while the three of us sit together at the breakfast table. He leans over and whispers, "There was a rumor going around that your mother died." He said.

"That must have been very upsetting to hear." I reply. I feel as though I'm speaking to a toddler. He scowls at me, unsure if I can be trusted. "Oh, I set them straight!" He snaps.

"Yeah, Mom's right here." I gesture to her with the spoon I'm using to feed her yogurt. He shakes his head at me. In his dementia he has once again become his angry abusive self. And I've become the imbecile daughter he believes has stolen his car. "That's not my wife." He says, shaking his head in annoyance.

Through the days, we go back in time to a place of exhaustion and stress, to a time before I was born, yet I am his daughter to him, still with my maiden name. How he can see me, his only daughter and youngest child, but he does not see this angel, this tiny bird of a woman sitting next to him as his wife? Nor can he see the fiftieth wedding anniversary that is approaching in four months and the way she carried him and his career and his life for five decades.

He can't remember that she taught us strength and perseverance in her own steadfast way, that she raised three kids on her own while he traveled for work. Nor can he remember how he softened through her diagnosis, that he

4

became a newer and kinder version of himself, rising to every occasion, visiting her every single day (twice a day) for six years into her dementia. He fed her ice cream, applied her lipstick, gave her kisses, teased "pull my finger" jokes and told her stories long after she was mute and unresponsive. It might be lost on him, but those truths will never leave me.

I want to write and I want to keep myself from writing. I want to see and I don't want to look. So I stare at the wreckage until I find beauty. There is a god, there is no god. I feel loves presence deeply, even while feeling deeply alone.

I want to study this, devour every word written on the subject. Absorbing myself in this paradoxical thinking, holding those opposing ideas in my mind at the same time.

This is Zen, this is bullshit.

This is the study of letting go.

The incremental death of both parents, yes.

And the complicated grief that accompanies life.

Chapter Two
July 2016

I'm not a doctor, but I google "hip labral tear" and determine this to be my diagnosis, for the hip that just won't behave itself in yoga class.

I'm not a doctor, but the past six months of parental health crisis have opened my eyes to the importance of finding a doctor when there's a health concern nagging at me. And my right hip is concerning me, so this freelance writer conjures up health insurance for the first time in fifteen years so I can get some answers to my limited mobility.

I mention my hip in passing, how it feels like there's a tennis ball in the hinge of a door, how it's getting harder to cross my leg on that side. And now the tennis ball is all I feel, while in Crescent Lunge position in yoga.

She's new to town, and this is our first appointment, so

this is just a meet and greet. "Maybe you can check out my hip next time I see you." I casually toss this idea out there, trying to be nonchalant.

She looks at me and smiles.

"Well, why don't I just check it out now?"

She's the doctor, I am not. So I hop onto the exam table. I'm still wearing my linen pants and Birkenstocks, because there's still nothing to worry about as she palpates my hip.

There's a brief second just before her expression changes. She looks up and I want her face to stay the same, to be casual. She's all business, but her eyes give her away.

"This isn't normal." she says.

"Let me make a phone call."

Do I say ok? Sure? No problem?

Am I even breathing?

She dials the phone on the wall and speaks clearly before hanging up. "You need to have an X-ray immediately."

It's 5pm on a Friday and this suddenly feels urgent. I comply dutifully and walk down an empty corridor to radiology, thinking maybe now would be a good time to start praying. In my hand I held a piece of paper that stated

My age: 41

My name: Meredith Winn

My diagnosis: Neoplasm of Uncertain Behavior.

Neoplasm of Uncertain Behavior is the technical term. The vague label they use when it's definitely something but it's too early to give you a solid diagnosis. A neoplasm: a new and abnormal growth of tissue in some part of the body, especially as a characteristic of cancer. Uncertain Behavior: a legitimate and specific pathologic diagnosis, a lesion whose behavior cannot be predicted. Malignant or benign? Cancer or not? The final behavior cannot be determined because the cells may be undergoing transformation as we speak. Uncertain behavior becomes my unpredictable existence.

I was late to my mother-in-law's backyard birthday party because I had just been on the X-ray table, resulting in my shadow of a health concern that could no longer be ignored.

I tried my best, because I was raised to make myself small and quiet and not be an inconvenience to anyone. So, I put on my party face, white as a ghost, at the picnic table decorated with lobster and corn on the cob, happy dogs running free and children laughing with summertime antics. I'm sure I carried on conversations, although I don't remember how I could have done so.

Only later, when we are alone, do I lean into his chest and cry in the driveway. He was disbelieving, as any fiancé would be. I have to say it again, so he understands.

"It's a tumor. They don't know if it's cancer yet, I need to have more tests." I pause and my words hover above our bodies. "I definitely need to have surgery before it breaks through my pelvic bone."

8

I'm unable to stop the tears now and feel as though I may puke. Right here on the dirt driveway. Right where my son learned to ride his bike just four years ago.

Steve continues holding me, and I feel guilty for bringing this reality to our life. I swallow audible sobs, unable to speak. His response is unflinching, as his steadfast and loving gaze meets my ugly cry.

"This will only make us stronger." He says.

"This will only make us more badass."

This is not my only story.

It does not define me.

And yet it is a part of me now.

Chapter Three

I'm not above striking a deal with my dying father. If there's any magic you can work from the other side, it would be greatly appreciated. It's a tumor, I know that and nothing else. I have a million questions and concerns. I want nothing more than to have a long life, to experience old age and snow white hair tied back in braids. I want to watch our three boys grow into adulthood.

But I'm on the phone with my father's nurse, signing the forms to get him on hospice. I am on the phone with my father's attorney. What happens to my mother when he dies? He was supposed to outlive her. "I'm advising you now, as your parents attorney." He speaks with authority and I feel more like a child than ever before, wanting desperately to hide behind my mother's skirt.

"We need to start this court process immediately."

"You'll become your mother's legal guardian."

"It's what your father would have wanted." He says.

Everything is unraveling. What do I believe anymore? I live prayer. Daily. It's the lazy woman's prayer: witnessing the wind in the leaves, the hawk circling above like a deep exhale. It's bare feet on soft moss, whispered words, astral projections and the reminder of magic. And sometimes in the dark of night, it's in the release of orgasm and tears.

Life is prayer. Breath is prayer. The test is to skate along the edge of death while contemplating life. To turn tragedy into triumph. Please don't be cancer. Please don't be cancer.

What is there to say? I think of what my mother would have said to me, if only she had the words in the early days of her diagnosis. But she couldn't pull herself together to discuss it, and I hated her for that. Yet here I am, unable to discuss my own diagnosis with my own family, and I run through all the excuses to justify my reasons.

"I love you", she would have said.

"I'll miss you." she would have said.

I'm realizing that through this vagueness, I am working out my own grief as I project an unknown future onto my son. The imaginary conversation I picture us having is what instantly bring me to tears. "You're the best thing that's ever happened to me." I'd say this on repeat until the end of time.

I have conversations in my head because I'm unable to

form words that reach Colorado where he spends his summer with his dad. I have conversations in my head because in reality, I am unable to form the words at all. My mouth just won't do it. When I look into the unknown future, in this period of waiting for test results, I don't know what to picture aside from a bone tumor. So, I picture a scar; and me, thankful for it.

I just removed four earrings, five rings and a toe ring that I haven't taken off my right foot in twenty years. A toe ring I bought myself in Taos, New Mexico, while working at a solar festival with my son's father. I thought I knew everything back then, I wrote bad fiction and never used my own voice. I could have never foreseen a future where I might lose my entire right leg.

I'm inside a tube, inside a trailer, in the parking lot of my small town hospital. Seventy-five minutes of MRI is enough for one lifetime. And now it's two days until my doctor has results that inform me of the next step.

Funny how until recently I never felt anything, I never had pain, only limited mobility. Now it seems like every little thing I feel, I feel in my pelvic bone. It resonates sound and vibration. It's the telltale heart, beating my fear from under the floorboards.

There's still so much living yet to be done. I want to float in water all across the world. I want to see Greece and Italy and France. I haven't even seen the world, and this thought makes me incredibly sad.

So, I picture a scar on my hip as I float, because that's me picturing myself alive in this world in the future.

The phone rings while we're driving to the coast. Bluetooth sends the call through the radio speakers and suddenly my primary care doctor is sitting in the car with us. Steve and I are heading to our sailboat off the coast of Portland. I pull over into the parking lot so I can focus on words, while my doctor goes over the radiologist results from my MRI. She can only confirm that I have a bone tumor.

"That's all we know." She says.
"We need more tests."
I'm left with the same information as before.
It might (or might not) be cancerous.
It's too soon to tell.

She's talking gently, letting me know that the next step is to meet with an orthopedic oncologist and they'll take a bone biopsy to determine if it's just a regular old bone tumor (best scenario) or a slow growing bone cancer (second best scenario) or a fast growing bone cancer (worst scenario). It's located on my pelvic bone, she tells me, connected with a small stem on the pelvis, but the tumor grows larger where it resides in my inner thigh.

She's tossing words out that I'm struggling to comprehend. "It's not common." she says, "I've never seen this before." Then for added emphasis she tells me, "We

13

learned about this in med school, for like, maybe thirty minutes." She ends the call in a way that I can't seem to shake, she gives me her personal cell phone number and says I can call her anytime. I get the sense that she's handing me off to a new set of specialists and I wonder if I'll actually ever see her again. I say thank you, and hang up.

We drive around the corner in silence for a solid minute before my phone rings again. Bluetooth speakers invite my father's hospice nurse into the car with us, she's letting me know my Dad is now transitioning to active death and it all seems to be happening fast. "I know you'd like to be here with him as he passes." she says, gently. The light turns red and I ball my fists hard into my eye sockets.

"This is too much, Mere." Steve says.
I continue staring straight ahead.
Just keep driving. Just make it to the coast.
Just keep going until you reach safety.
Just get to home base.

The sand, the sea, the edge of the earth. The place where you used to find safety in your mother's hand, her grip so tight you knew she'd never let you go. You drive to where she taught you to jump in the waves at high tide. It is, ultimately, the place where you finally end up unravelling completely.

Chapter Four

Today's sounds from the coast of Maine are there to soothe the void, to hush the migraine, to lighten the load. I wake at 4:30am to watch the sunrise off our boat and make a note to self: there is joy here, on earth, in this life. I want to always remember that.

I keep swimming in healing waters, not knowing how to pray. Please let me live. I repeat in my head. I don't pray, I beg; greedy for more life. I want more time, more love, more more more.

I become superstitious of words and phrases used in my presence. I'm a micro-manager, prone to correcting Steve's speech so as not to jinx my future with him, and he graciously listens to me even though I've lost my mind.

"It's not *if* but *when*." I say.

I coach him in proper terminology, grammar, dialect.
"*When* we get married. *When* we see the world.
When we live a long life together."

It's hope and faith. And I am blindly searching for signs
of any god that may exist and have my back on this. Please.
Let. Me. Live. I really truly love my life. I'm not ready for it
to be over yet.

My phone rings, after watching the early sunrise, it's
9am and my favorite nurse from the nursing home is on the
other end of the line. She's calling me from Virginia.
"Meredith, his color has changed." She says.
"You need to get down here as soon as you can."
"He's dying."

I book a flight immediately from my phone. The soonest
flight leaves today from our tiny airport in Portland, Maine,
at 5pm. I pack my bag.
What are you supposed to bring with you to watch
your father die? I don't know how to do this. I don't know
anything anymore. I'm just going to sit at his bedside. I'm
just going to hold his hand as he dies. I don't know how to
be this brave.
On my way to the airport, I call my mother's hospice
nurse, to let her know when my flight will land. She's a
hospice nurse, but feels more like family after two years of
her bereavement support. My mother has been on hospice

16

for two years; and now this gentle woman helps guide me through my father's journey. She's a midwife for the dying and a tremendous support for the grieving family left behind.

It's true, death is a rite of passage that often goes unseen and is unspoken in our modern culture. Her voice is a comfort to me while I drive to the airport. And after we hang up, I drive in silence. Then clearly, as if he were riding shotgun right beside me, I hear my dad's voice.

"Say goodnight, Gracie." He says.

A favorite line of his, quoting George Burns, and spoken almost every night of my childhood. I haven't thought of this in more than twenty years.

Chapter Five

Dear Dad,

You died on a Sunday evening and I've never felt less brave and more sad. Is this the hardest thing to face? To hold. To accept. To witness vulnerability, to receive love graciously, to provide comfort and dignity and to continue loving through loss? And somehow through that emptiness, love more deeply?

No one knows what to say, including myself. I have no words, just a million tears as my heart swims through the atmosphere in slow motion. How are any of us standing? How are any of us loving, living, breathing, surviving? I'm in awe of the resiliency of the human heart.

I'm about to board the plane when my phone rings. I'm at the gate. It doesn't make sense. He can't be dead.

"Can you hear me?" She asks.

He was supposed to wait for me to get there.

"Do you understand?" She asks again.

They say they can hold his body for me, for when I arrive. After two planes and airport delays; I make phone calls, loudly and publicly, with incoherent words slobbering from my mouth. After so many tissues and swollen eyes, I think I am prepared to see his body, so I tell them yes, hold his body for me.

My mother's best friend picks me up at the airport, it's well after 10pm and I know she must be exhausted. I cry in her car as she drives through the dark. As my "other mother" she makes this suggestion, offering to come inside with me.

"I don't want you to do this alone." She says.

I'm thankful to be mothered by her. She is my mother's doppelgänger. A naval officer's wife, same as my mom, and a New Englander through and through; wearing stylish Capri pants and fashionable jewelry, they must have had a real hoot together.

Damn, I miss my mom. Being around her best friend is almost exactly like being around my mom, so I do as I am told. And we walk inside the nursing home together.

My favorite nurse meets me inside at 11pm, long after she went home for the day. She got out of bed, she said, because she didn't want me to be there alone with an unfamiliar night staff.

"I need to warn you, Meredith..."

"He's been gone for five hours." She says.

"His body is starting to change." She says.

I meet her eye. She mentions the word "grey" and I feel nauseous. I walk into my mother's room, and see my mom sleeping, curled into fetal position. In the twin bed opposite my mothers, is the body of my father, lying prone.

It's as if there is a forcefield around his bed, and it keeps me from getting close. I simply cannot move my feet in his direction. He looks nothing like my father, this body is empty and waxy and yes, grey. This was once my father. But my father is gone.

I find safety on my mother's side of the room. Strange as that is to say, because she is slowly dying, but right now she is warm and living. Her oxygen tank clicks and breathes and mutters to me the sad story of her life.

Alive. Alive. Alive, it says.

End-of-life Dementia, it says.

And I am at once so very sad for her, that her husband of fifty years has died and she didn't get to say goodbye.

And neither did I.

At the nurses station, calls have been made to the funeral home, and it's been suggested that I don't stay to witness them arrive to move his body.

I nod and follow every suggestion.

I am a child, a forty-one year old baby.

I am obedient and silent.

20

A petite woman in scrubs comes up to me, reaching out to hug me. I've known her through the years.

She is crying. I tower over her.

I'm a stone statue unable to cry.

"I was with him." She says. "I wheeled Mama into the dining room. But she refused to eat dinner tonight. I'm sure that she knew, in her own way, that he passed."

"He waited for her to leave the room, then took his last breath." I take in that visual. My father alone.

Waiting for privacy. As he lived, he died.

"In my culture, we open the window for the soul to be free." She says. "I opened the window for him." She says, and it's the sweetest thing I've tasted all day.

Before I leave to sleep in my parents empty house, I am handed a phone. He introduces himself as the funeral director, explaining that we will meet in the morning but he'd like to ask a few questions tonight. His Southern accent is so sticky, I cannot understand a single word he's saying. I ask him to repeat himself. I'm on another planet, where his words don't match my vocabulary. He's trying to gather necessary information from me.

"I don't understand," I say.

He needs to transport my fathers body.

"I don't understand," I repeat.

My favorite nurse takes the phone from me

I sit down blinking.

Where am I? How did I get here?

The 2am phone call I place to my sister-in-law is mostly incoherent. She receives me with tenderness while I fumble and stammer through shock. I'm on autopilot and my headlights are leading me down the road, through my parents neighborhood, where I learned to drive at age fifteen.

"His body was grey," I say.

"He was gone," I say.

"It wasn't him," I say.

"I don't know what I believe anymore," I say.

Chapter Six

There are two words I hear myself say on repeat the morning after my father died: Thank You.

Thank You is said over and over again to strangers, to friends, to the wind and the sun. And then later, well after meeting funeral directors in quiet offices, making arrangements and signing paperwork while in business mode (ankles crossed, pen in hand, choosing urns).

Only then, in the quiet dark of bedtime, while my mother sleeps just a few feet away, I pack up my dad's belongings and clothes from the room they shared. The sight of his shoes in the empty space where he once slept, became the hard reality of this day.

It's his Adidas sneakers that finally make me cry.

My father died and I am finding it's the small things make me jumpy and scared, like a little kid, unsure. The lightening of a storm, usual things that wouldn't have phased me much. A dog barking at the end of his chain, lunging as dogs do; but me, frozen for a moment and then panicky.

I wonder if there's an energetic discharge of some sort, when a parent dies. The untethering of a cord. Or if it's just grief in general. I feel as though I'm walking around without skin and everything is getting in.

Apparently in my (grief) or (insomnia) or (disorientation) or (simply a combination of any of those three) I send emails and texts, rambling books of an ongoing dialogue I'm carrying on in my delusion.

These are threads connecting myself and my inner circle of people across the miles. I don't know where one ends and the other picks up. I'm tired of hearing my own voice. I'm tired of the voices in my head. I'm tired of crying, thinking the well surely has run dry, only to find more tears in unexpected places.

Kneeling at the foot of my mother's wheelchair with my head in her lap; loud, audible and uncontrollable tears are shared with nurses. I find comfort in that. They apologize for their lack of professionalism, when the business face slips into tears; but I only cry *Thank You*, it's no burden on me. Sharing grief makes me feel less alone.

They wake my mother at the same time every day. Bathe her while she's still in bed, with wet wipes or a wash cloth, after her diaper change. Then they use a Hoyer Lift,

24

a hospital crane, to physically move her from her bed to wheelchair. She curls like a baby in the hammock of this contraption and opens her eyes for a brief second.

When the motion feels like a swing, her mouth opens and I wonder if she remembers being an infant. I wonder if she remembers her own mother's love. When dementia leaves you with nothing but sunlight and shadows, I pray that love is all to remain.

I comb her hair, and she keeps her eyes closed. I wheel her to the dining room to feed her yogurt. Last time I sat here, I fed both of my parents. The seat next to me is now empty, and every nurse on the morning shift has been briefed with the news from the night. There was a death: Amity's husband has died.

My mother has lived in this facility the longest. She's miraculously outlived everyone else. They refer to her affectionately as "Am" or "Mama" and she's the baby, the sweetheart, the shell of a woman who has not spoken, walked, or fed herself for many years. The nurses come to the breakfast table one by one, and offer condolences, while I feed my mom. She instinctively opens her mouth like a baby bird waiting to receive food.

"Thank you," I say to them all.
"I love you," I say to her again and again.
Thank you, I love you. It's all that matters.

25

Chapter Seven

Once a day since my dad died, I have laughed so hard I've cried. Life is so fucking tragic. Yet funny. Like this email from my father's friend and former co-worker, a well respected man, clearly sent from his iPhone that reads:

"You have my deepest symphony."

That autocorrect couldn't have been more inappropriate (or mortifying for him) but so perfectly fitting. I laughed so hard I had to sit down weeping.

I was a classically trained clarinetist; and every week throughout high school, my father would drive me to my symphony practice in the next town over. I'd leave his car with my clarinet in hand, smelling like his cigar smoke.

"You have my deepest symphony."

I have to tell my mom that dad died. I know she knows this, somewhere deep in her psyche; she may not understand anything other than a shift of energy, but she knows. So I am just confirming her loss. After lunch, I wheel her to the ice cream social, the daily entertainment that my father so enjoyed with her. Socializing plus sweets? He ate ice cream every single day.

They scoop my mother chocolate, on a cone, because the one thing she is still able to do, is hold an ice cream cone and eat it like a toddler. I sit beside her, watching other families, watching other nurses go about their business. And I catch the eye of my father's favorite nurse. She's tough as nails and that's why he loved her more than anyone here. She comes over and puts her hand on my shoulder.

"How ya doing?" she asks, and I burst into tears.

"My dad loved feeding her ice cream." I say

"This is so fucking hard for me." I say.

She hugs me, and tells me to go wash my face.

Ice cream drips down Mom's chin and onto her bib.

Three days after my father's death, the dreams begin.

He is here, there, asking me about the diagnosis that I didn't have time to share with him before he died. The diagnosis that feels like a punch to the gut, even while in dream state. And then his solid presence in my dreams, as if I am awake, and he's asking me if my bone tumor is causing me pain. His genuine concern is felt, like a father's love, like talking to him each morning on the phone. There he was, as if alive; with a kiss on my cheek before waking.

In my dreams I walk at full speed, with huge strides. I feel the wind on my face and I'm faster than cars on the road. Sometimes in my dreams my dad walks with me; like Laverne and Shirley, and our legs kick out as we goof on down the sidewalk, just as they did in the tv shows we watched together. Just like the family walks from my childhood each night after the Carol Burnett show and before The Muppets.

Shlemiel, Schlimazel, Hasenpfeffer Incorporated.

And so comes the practice: to celebrate the spirit, honor life and allow death to come to the dying. The veil between worlds is silky like a soft gauze that allows in the light.

Chapter Eight

I talk to his urn.

It's heavier than I thought it would be. He rides shotgun and I've tidied up the car so he won't look disapprovingly at me over the top of his glasses, judging my messy road trip car interior. There's a fine layer of dust on top of the urn and I run my finger through it, leaving a smudge. I drive away without buckling him in.

Life is just weird, man. That's all. How his house feels empty in a strange way, and his ashes and dust are just there sitting on his recliner as I empty out his fridge and pantry, filling boxes and bags to donate to the food bank. He was a Navy Officer and kept his pantry in shipshape: row after row of mushroom Alfredo pasta sauce.

My mom kept her eyes closed all day except for about two minutes when I first got there. She's been reaching out for my hand constantly and then won't easily let go of it. When I pry her fingers off me, to push her wheelchair, she's almost like a frantic baby, reaching out into space for something she senses to be there. Her fingers are very busy, rubbing my hands, pinching my rings and holding my bracelets.

She's doing this whisper thing, a very guttural whisper where her mouth is moving. She hasn't spoken in years, but it's almost as if she's communicating, or praying, or channeling the dead. I spend hours sitting with her, holding her hand, kissing her forehead and cheeks. I sing and hum, off key, as she did for me when I was young.

It's going to be ok. It has to be. And everything that needs to happen, will happen. I have to trust this with my whole being although it feels like a foreign mantra I've adopted. Believing in stardust and sprites, while I have a real mass, a softball size tumor, growing inside of me. I can't bear leaving my mom alone but I need to get home for my next doctor's appointment.

I keep thinking about how my father was maybe not really the dad I needed growing up, but it's the dad I got. From behind this wall there is infrequent and unexplainable emotion, wrought with missing. For what never was. And for the glimpse I got of him in his later, more tender years.

Everyone is telling me what a kind man he was. And how he was so proud of me. How he shared every single piece of writing I ever had published, and how he'd make xerox copies and hand them out to anyone willing to read my words. I know this about him, but the ghosts of our dysfunction still haunt me from the years he had long ago forgotten. He did his best, as any of us can do.

"I'll be back after I feed Mom dinner!"

I say this out loud to no one other than a metal urn sitting on a leather recliner, where my father used to sit and doze and watch tv too loud as the old man once was.

Chapter Nine

Dear Dad, While cleaning out dressers and making piles of white undershirts to donate to the thrift store, I came across a birthday card you wrote to mom last year. Six years after her diagnosis and many many years since she's uttered your name, let alone an entire sentence. It was a card you wrote to her and read to her, your shaky handwriting no longer masking your emotion and love for this woman.

Just shy of fifty years of marriage.

You died 28 days before her birthday.

I'm trying to remember the last words you said to me and I'm drawing a blank. I remember kissing your forehead and saying *I love you*. I told you *Be good* (the phrase most commonly said by you my entire life) the same two words you'd say when hanging up the phone, the two words uttered when you could not say *I love you* because men of your generation where raised differently. *Be good* was the phrase to guide the good girl, the obeyer, the pleaser in me.

Hey Dad, I caught a man's reflection in the mirror the other day, he was about your age. The entire room reminded me of you, not so much the exercise bikes or the staff to assist, but the man himself. Not so much his jeans and Adidas sneakers or even his old man mannerisms.

It was the reflection in the mirror, it was how the physical therapist gently held onto the back of his belt loop. Just as your therapist and nurses did for you.

When I emptied your closet and bagged up your clothes to donate, mom slept in the very same room. Your side of the room now empty while her oxygen tank whirred and gasped like an asthmatic, clicking away all night for her added comfort. It was your broken belt loops that tossed me over the edge - straight into a dark and deep pool of grief.

Every belt loop on the back of your jeans was torn from all the help you needed in those final weeks and days of your life. When grabbing and holding you up by your armpits wasn't enough anymore for a nurse on either of your arms, one was needed in the back too, on the belt loop to guide your bottom down into the wheelchair. To act as a lifeline, as if that small piece of denim fabric would hold your body weight should your legs go out from under you when the strokes caught up with your muscles and mobility.

We all put our trust and belief in that single belt loop. I'm not sure how it's possible that all men over the age of seventy-five become you; but I wonder where their daughters are now, and if they called to hear a father's voice each week. If they are able to move past the differences to finally come to a place of peace.

The vacancy of death in the physical world does not mean our work is done. We are still connected. You are everywhere. And I'm open to what you have learned in your time away. I hope you are free from unhappiness.

I'm sitting next to a woman my age and her father. This guy reminds me of you, too, but the old man version of you, when we found ourselves navigating the world together in your last year of life and I accompanied you to doctor appointments. This man calls his daughter "darling" and that's a kind word that never crossed your lips. You were many things, but you were not kind.

I keep remembering that last appointment, when you received your vascular dementia diagnosis and how angry you were with me. And how you let everyone know it too, with rude gestures and spitting words. I knew your reality was slipping from you then and in your mind I was the angsty teen. You were lost somewhere twenty-four years earlier when I wrecked mom's car at age 17.

These moments pop into my mind in the most unusual of places. I smile at this woman with the funky sneakers and edgy haircut, her father in a short sleeve polo just like you used to wear. It's easy to smile and picture them perfect, but the reality is that relationships are challenging. No one on the outside knows what's going on within that inner dynamic.

I'm sorry, Dad. I'm sorry that mom got sick and your world fell apart. I'm sorry that your last year of life was so frustrating for you. I know it was scary and you were unable to vocalize this. I'm sorry for your anger and harsh words spoken with venom in public. I'm sorry. And I forgive you.

We did the best we could.

Chapter Ten

I had to sell your car, Dad. And I keep feeling like that's wrong, like you will come back and need it and be ultimately pissed at me. But you're dead. And you stated in your will that it needed to be sold.

It's these irrational jags in perception that throw me. Sideswiped by emotion and blindsided by the reality that hits hard on busy days, when the mail piles up with my parents bills, overdue and unopened. And there's my ceaseless excuse again, the one I've quickly grown tired of hearing.

"I'm sorry." I say.

"The past month has been a blur." I say.

I've learned about the silence that comes from the other end of the phone line: his internet company, credit card companies, and insurance companies all pause briefly as they begin to read the bereavement script.

All those kind strangers trained to work in the bereavement department of their corporation, they still seem unsure of what to make of this story I'm concocting. I keep thinking this must be some mistake. My father didn't die, but I notified all his friends, printed an obituary in the newspaper, and worst of all: cremated his body.

This is some terrible mistake; I certainly won't have this rare type of cancer. But I google the name of my orthopedic oncologist just to make sure he is real.

"What a head fuck!"

I keep saying to anyone who won't be offended.

"I had a dream that my father faked his own death just to escape a tax on his estate."

Grief brings about a very physical confusion, a living nightmare where my mom comes jogging out of her front door (the house I'm obligated to empty of its contents and then sell). But through the haze, there she is wearing her favorite floral pants standing next to the car telling me to "hustle" while clapping her hands like a cheerleader, just as she did when I was young.

Now his body is nothing but dust and I have, in my wallet, the transit permit allowing me to bring his cremated remains across state lines.

Is it possible that I feel his presence in his ashes?

Even when I feel his presence in my dreams?

His favorite Hawaiian shirt, his mischievous grin. If he's here, he's everywhere. I drive fifteen hours straight, from his house in Virginia to my house in Maine. What am I running from? What am I running towards?

I won't open my father's urn. I set him on the floor of my bedroom. Steve and I walk around him, pile bills on him, stub our toes on him in the dark of night. I am utterly disrespectful in my disconnect, in my avoidance, with my fingers in my ears: LaLaLaLaLa.

I'm home for a single day before Steve and I drive to the border of New Hampshire and Vermont. The Green Mountains are beautiful in summer and Dartmouth Hospital is home to a Sarcoma Program, where I'll have a series of painful bone biopsies and then wait for results to determine my diagnosis and subsequent surgery date.

One thing at a time, girlie, and remember to eat.

We find ourselves a pizza place, after walking around the quaint campus of an Ivy League College. It's open mic night, and there's a table of musicians with fiddles and guitars. I don't know if I eat dinner, or if I even carried on a normal conversation with Steve, but I do remember the little old man with the banjo at the restaurant. And how I cried at our table, watching him shuffle to his feet in saggy jeans and suspenders. I do remember his expression changing, lighting up, when he was asked to join the group; and how his grandkids needed to help him up out of his chair.

38

God damn, the tenderness of life.

I want to live just to see more of this.

When I am angry or bitterness threatens to swallow me in darkness, remind me of the eighty-five year old woman I met only once when I was very young. Her mother was my Grandmother's best friend, making her and my father nearly cousins or siblings, depending on the mood.

Remind me that she reached out to me, through all of this death and illness. Remind me that she said, *Grace and strength*, Meredith. Remind me that she said she hasn't been to church in quite some time because she fears she's angry with God; because she doesn't understand his ways.

God damn, the tenderness of life.

I want to live just to experience more of this honesty.

Chapter Eleven

It doesn't seem real, because the two most important people you cry too when you have cancer are your parents. And they were the only two people I was not able to tell. It felt surreal, and wrong, and full of mistake and sadness.

My reality and dream state are mixing and it's making me say sincerely naïve things like, *I don't understand your question,* to the small town librarian, to the grocery store cashier, to the woman sticking me with a needle to draw blood for the hundredth time.

A general state of confusion:

That's what they should call cancer.

Without suffering, we cannot truly live.

Is this Buddhism?

Because it feels like bullshit.

Fourteen days until my son comes home from his summer away. I miss him so much. I'm also terrified of what I need to tell him.

He calls on FaceTime. I'm in a hotel room not far from Dartmouth-Hitchcock Medical Center, having just cried myself sick after being diagnosed with a rare pelvic bone cancer. The tumor is malignant and the size of a softball. There will be a tumor board meeting of sarcoma specialists to discuss my case study. We are advised to stay in town and not drive three hours home, so I can meet with specialists again in the morning.

There's a sudden urgency, like life is in crisis. Yet my feet move slowly like the earth is grabbing hold of my ankles, ready to drag me to the underworld.

My son doesn't question why I'm under the sheet of a hotel bed, or why my eyes are red-rimmed. He's wearing a huge rubber kitty mask that he saved up his allowance for. He's eleven; proud of his dry sense of humor and the way he makes me laugh. We've been doing these summers away for eight years now, it's hard to believe.

We've missed each other so much this summer and can't wait to see each other. He says he's sad about his Pop-Pop dying. He asks how Nana is doing, if she understands death.

My son's young life has been lived in the shadow of illness. Accidentally, of course. Because no one wants a three year old to learn about dementia, but there's simply no avoiding it when a grandmother becomes cognitively younger than him before his very own eyes.

He's grown up in the shadow of death, unable to read *Owl Babies* or *Are You My Mother?* because his worst unspoken fear was mother loss. Back when he refused to hold his Nana's hand, because he thought dementia was contagious. "Her brain is sick." Is how I explained it to him at age four. He grew wise beyond his years, through the early stages of her illness. And I will always feel that part of his childhood was robbed from him.

After hanging up the phone, I am once again wondering how the fuck I'm going to explain my cancer to this fresh young soul. And I just can't wrap my head around it.

Chapter Twelve

This was supposed to be our summer of live music. It's surreal now, sitting outside with these tickets purchased so many months ago, long before death and cancer.

He leans in to kiss me and it's a sunhat collision with my best friend, my lover, my partner in life. I met him when I was thirty-six. Let's grow old together, ok? Let's have forty more years of silliness and love and life. Let's get through this and continue raising our boys together. Let's see the world. Let's live and live and live.

I pray harder than I've ever prayed. Music becomes prayer, blasting loud in the car. And live music becomes church, blasting in my ears.

The good news came back with my PET scan: my cancer has not spread to my lymph nodes nor metastasized to my lungs. The good news came back with my MRI's, CT scans, X-rays and bone biopsies: it's a low grade Sarcoma.

Chondrosarcoma is a rare form of bone cancer (of the cartilage) and while the tumor is supposedly the size of a softball, it's contained to my pelvic bone. This type of Sarcoma is not receptive to chemotherapy or radiation, so surgery is the only option for survival.

The good news came back that I will get to keep my leg, that modern medicine is now able to perform limb-salvaging surgery. An internal amputation, called a hemipelvectomy. And while they will remove part of my pelvis, I am fully expected to recover and learn to walk again.

Steve sat beside me while my oncologist explains all of this in detail and I blink and nod, while tears stream down my face. "Oh, you're going to make me cry," my favorite nurse comments with such tenderness.

"Meredith's dad just died this week."

Steve explains my silence to the room.

There is no correct way to be human anymore.

I am completely detached.

My dad always appreciated a well placed F-bomb. And there have been plenty of them this week. I'm currently reconstructing my reality.

I hate you, cancer. And yet apparently, my doctor thinks I grew you unknowingly, for years and years and years. Possibly since a rapid growth spurt in my teenage years.

What a total headfuck. My body has betrayed me.
All the while sweet talking me, just to get in my pants.

I will not be angry with god, the universe, the karmic wheel or the divine plan. I will trust and believe in the power of love. My heart will not turn to a small bitter stone. And I will continue to say thank you, for the rest of my days.

May it be so.

Chapter Thirteen

Blood type: O Positive
Oh! Positive!

I'm just not ready to even talk about it, but surgery is four days away. I've decided to be a fucking coward and not even use the word Cancer. My hope is that my surgery deems me cancer-free and alive, and so I'll cross that bridge of explanation (in a wheelchair) when I get to it.

Are there books on how to tell your child that you have cancer? I don't know. Maybe there are, but I don't even ask google to search for one because I'm in denial. Also, who the fuck would write that book?

Not only am I in denial, I'm also very angry. How can I make my mouth form the words they are refusing to say?

Am I just an overprotective mother? Perhaps. Am I being selfish? Possibly. Am I lost in grief? Definitely. Am I acting out of self preservation with the deepest love for this family of mine? The same blended family that teeters on splinters and melancholy? Totally.

We both make the parental executive decision to tell our three boys (my son and two future stepsons) a Little Big White Lie. And it's a pill they swallow easily, because, you know, we totally downplay it. Pretty much, we lie. I guess if there's a Hell, I'll burn in it.

Yes, I'm having mother guilt over my inability to handle this appropriately. But there's only so much fucking grief one family needs to experience this month.

"I need surgery on my hip." I say.

My new mantra: Surgery and Cancer-free.

I make Steve lists inside a pink notebook. Words go unspoken between us, but he knows it's in case I don't wake up. In case I die.

The list includes the people to call. It includes all my mother's information; medical and financial. She is seen as an incapacitated adult in the eyes of the court, and I am her guardian and conservator.

The notebook also stores an envelope labeled *in case of emergency* that holds a handwritten letter to my son, to be opened only upon my death. Steve is my next of kin, although we are not yet legally married. We've been engaged for four years. It never felt right to have a wedding my mother

47

couldn't attend. I show him how to forge my signature and access my bank account, so when my dad's life insurance check arrives in the mail, he knows what to do with it.

In case of emergency.
Get your affairs in order.

Chapter Fourteen

Four hours before surgery. Steve spoons me on a hotel bed, after I've washed from neck to toes with antiseptic soap. I text my best friend to tell her I love her. She provides me with my new mantra: Surrender.

The week my father died I was diagnosed with a rare bone cancer. I'm practicing saying this statement because it feels too true to be real. To unreal to be true.

The pre-surgery scrub they give you has a strong medical smell and I worry there's not enough of it, to wash my body from neck to ankles. In the bathroom mirror I see my reflection and for a split second I don't recognize myself.

My brave face: the mask I wear when I am scared out of my fucking mind. This is the face of fierce strength. Fierce love for everyone and everything.

This is the before. The night before the thirteen hour surgery that would remove a five inch section of my pelvic bone along with a tumor that ended up being the size of a grapefruit (lodged in my thigh).

This is the unknown. The letting go. The immense trust in steady hands and a team of surgeons that will become friends over the next ten years as they follow my health as a cancer survivor. This is me chanting *Surgery and Cancer-free*. Like a prayer, an Om, a mantra said while worshipping at the feet of the gods.

This is the face of a woman telling people she has "hip issues" because her mouth is not yet able to form the literal sentence, "I have bone cancer" to anyone who's not in the innermost circle of friends.

This is the heart not yet able to look three boys in the eye and whisper the truth at the kitchen table. This is me admitting I am the sheltering mask of overprotection from a reality I was not yet ready to face myself. A reality I was determined to beat like a motherfucker with or without the use of a god damned wheelchair, walker, crutches, and cane.

This is me and the 4am wake up call that found me kneeling on the cold hard hotel bathroom floor. Praying all prayers, for all time. Praying until my knees ached. Praying to a god I may or may not believe in anymore.

This is me, before 180 stitches. Before the battle scar of a cancer survivor. The face of a forty-one year old woman who never stopped saying thank you.

Part II

Chapter Fifteen

I find pages of notes, hidden on my phone with blurred memories of hospital beds and sleep lost to hallucinations. I mark the words I hear bounce round my head. They are my scratchings on the wall of the cave, depicting days spent on bedrest, in recovery.

This is the glow of the screen staring back at me from the Notes app on my iPhone. This is me numb from the chest down, pinned to the hospital bed with IV lines and tubes. My words were my only roommates aside from the morphine and fentanyl, aside from the hallucinations who took up real estate next to the very real Steve who sat by my bed.

I made the doctors promise me I wouldn't wake up an amputee. I made them sign a paper, so if the tumor was larger than they thought and they needed to take my entire leg, they'd have to wake me up and tell me first. They entertained me by signing it, while reminding me that this had only happened once in their experience.

And still the panic attack swallowed me, after thirteen hours under anesthesia, I was gulping air, thinking *Oh fuck! The pain! Oh fuck!* And the blurry man holding my oxygen mask laughs in my direction.

"I've heard much worse," he says,
He turns to another blurry person in scrubs.
Asking him, "What's for dinner?"
There's a pause while I wonder if it's mid-day.
If they need to amputate my leg.
 "It's 6pm" he says.
"Your surgery is over."
Oh my god. Thank you for my legs!

The things they must hear when patients are ripped from anesthesia back to the land of the living; unable to fall on the ground kissing the earth, so glad to feel pain like bolts of lightening, so completely surprised to be alive.

Chapter Sixteen

In the moments before surgery everyone comes to meet me. My orthopedic oncology team (4-5 people), a vascular team of plastic surgeons (4-5 people), an anesthesiologist, and a pain management team.

Surgeons and doctors will blur into many faces, those who will stand over my body for hours upon hours and open my pelvis with sterilized sharp instruments, doctors who will break bone with saws and mallets and hammers, doctors that will carry a tumor down to pathology then stop to speak with Steve in the waiting room. Doctors that will sever nerves and cut muscles and move them to new locations, doctors that will sew me together with precision and silk.

That moment before surgery, Steve is by my side until the very end of the hallway, when they tell me they can give me something to calm my nerves. They wheel me after saying goodbye to him, the last thing I see is the person I love. I don't remember how we parted, or the words we shared.

The fluid they call a "happy cocktail" goes in my IV port and one moment I'm there, and the next I'm gone. It's frightening how eager I am to leave my body. They must have moved me like a rag doll, rolling me on my side to insert the needle into my spine. Spreading my legs to shave and catheter me. Wheeling me to a room where I lay with eyes closed for thirty minutes while the start time was delayed and doctors gathered themselves and the tools needed for a limb salvage surgery.

The moments leading up to surgery were all a blur except for the green sharpie. He was the plastic surgeon with the eastern European accent and excellent hair, the man who carried a green sharpie in the breast pocket of his scrubs.

He started drawing lines to mark the leg for surgery.

X's were drawn first: five of them in total.

The first X marked the outer thigh of the right leg. I'll learn later that this first X marked the Lateral Femoral Cutaneous Nerve that they would need to sever, which would leave my right thigh numb for the rest of my life. A second X is drawn on the site of the tumor located on my Pubis Bone. Out comes the Doppler that allows him to listen to the pulse in my thigh. And a third X is placed dead center, in the spot I would later learn is where they took my skin graft (or "the flap" as my medical team will disgustingly referred it).

Another listen with the Doppler and a fourth X is marked above my knee cap (which still remains numb to this day). The fifth X is drawn at the top of my foot, at the Dorsalis Pedis Artery, a location from where they can take a pulse.

Now with five X's on me, he draws a line down the length of me, from pelvis to thigh to kneecap, connecting three of these X's with a green line that was not straight. This bothered me, its asymmetrical non-straightness.

He saw my face grimace in judgment.

"That's not a cut line," He said.

"This is like a roadmap."

It wouldn't be until two days later, when the nurses pulled back the sheet and the doctor took my bandages off, that I saw it actually *was* the cut line. I tried not to fixate on its crookedness. It was hard to navigate this roadmap, this new leg. Where was my knee? My hip? Whose skin was this on my thigh? Where have my freckles gone?

Sutures tied me together at the seams with "the flap" sitting like a three inch wide boomerang across my bikini line and down my thigh. Where did that skin come from? I'm a patchwork quilt.

I'm fucking Frankenstein.

The boomerang shaped skin looks vaguely familiar to me. But I didn't know what I was looking at; my leg was not my leg anymore. It wasn't until later that I realized the freckles that had once danced across my thigh were now sitting on the skin graft that covered my abdomen.

After the recovery room where I woke from anesthesia, I was wheeled to ICU where Steve fed me ice chips, although I remember nothing of this. Nurses can monitor my breathing here, and also monitor the "flap". They listen to my skin graft with the Doppler like I am a pregnant woman waiting to hear my unborn baby's heartbeat. But when the heartbeat sounds, it's the medical relief that blood is flowing, that the skin graft is alive and pumping with rerouted blood vessels.

ICU provides no memories for me except a vibe: a frantic energy, like a factory farm of hospital patients. Bed after bed, row after row, all lined up with machines between, and nurses bustling about.

I have no memory except for the beeping and the alarms. I am so completely fucked up on meds, but if only I could hit that snooze button, I'd be allowed some god damn peace to sleep for nine more minutes. My alarm was sounding because every few minutes I'd stop breathing, Steve tells me later. And the incessant beeping would shake me coherent and I'd take another breath. The moment of quiet provided just enough peace for me to slip away again. Just nine more minutes is all I wanted.

Apparently I told him I had flown myself to Hawaii, with my arms, like a bird; like the flying dreams of my childhood. Pausing only to rest and hang from telephone wires along the way, I flew like a bird across deep waters from the land of anesthesia. I also worked frantically, typing out emails and writing page after page on my laptop, as if my life depended on it. I told him this. That the place I had gone to was pain free, it was sunlit and pleasant. Time ellipses while on the other side and it was over before I knew it.

Thirteen hours of surgery had passed and I awoke with a jolt, like an engine catching spark and firing up for the first time after being forgotten in a weedy field, not remembering if it knew how to run.

My lungs filled for the first time without the use of breathing tubes and machines and I was ripped from sunlight into a world of pain.

I told Steve things I don't remember. He holds those pieces of my story now; he keeps them safe for me. It's unsettling, really, to think of my mouth forming words, my brain processing thoughts and actions; like a marionette, like a puppet going through the motions of limbs and speech.

Ah! So this is how we pretend to be human.

Chapter Seventeen

I wake up, neither day nor night. The curtain is pulled and a tv blasts from the other side of the room. I don't have a window, I have a view of the hallway and a glimpse of the bathroom that neither myself nor my roommate can physically use. I never see my roommate although I know she is female and her husband has a loud voice that makes the curtain move like a breeze through the window.

Nurses are busy, but one informs me that I have to call and order my own food. I have to read from a menu. I have to figure out how to dial a phone. I am medicated beyond belief and can't fathom that I've been trusted to be in charge of my own body's nourishment. I close my eyes and sleep. I don't know enough to feed myself. It's possible that someone feeds me yogurt. Or applesauce. I really don't know.

A short haired nurse sits beside my bed. Where's Steve? Is it night or early morning? Has he gone to the hotel to get some rest? She's young and finds herself holding my hand while I cry. I tell her my dad died and this hospital reminds me of him. She tells me she lost her dad too, about eight years ago and she thinks of him everyday.

"When did your dad die?"

She asks, accepting my melancholy.

"Last month," I say.

I see her sorrow bubble to the surface of her professionalism. She takes the phone from the nightstand and orders me breakfast, then brings a cup of water to my mouth and holds the straw for me. I am a 41 year old child who requires assistance. I'm lost in Sears Roebuck again, looking for my mom's familiar corduroy pants. My mother would tell this story again and again throughout her life; replaying her terror and how she alerted all workers and managers to search for me. Fight or flight or freeze. I had given up hope and curled myself into a ball in the rug department, waiting for someone to come rescue me.

I can't believe my luck.

I had bone cancer. I got to keep my leg. My roommate's leg was painfully shattered from a motorcycle accident. She's requiring emergency surgery to either attempt reconstruction or amputate her leg entirely. I look down at my two legs, one completely bandaged from belly to knee.

Life is pretty much the luck of the draw.

Chapter Eighteen

Is it evening now? Steve has advocated for me, behind the scenes, working his magic to get me a private room.

He was here? I don't remember.

Has he witnessed my spirit leaking onto the floor, in a puddle around the metal legs of my hospital bed? There are a thousand things I don't know. He stands beside me and my tears. My sadness has earned me a room of my own with a window and although I have no idea where I am, I know that I am moving rooms soon.

I see him walking towards me down a brightly lit hallway. The brim of his hat making a halo around his face. He's smiling and carrying a small bag from the hospital gift shop. He can't wait to show me the new pair of socks he bought me. Apparently every time the staff recommends I wear the hospital-issued-non-slip-standard-grey-socks that my dad had to wear in rehab, I burst into tears and refuse to wear them. So, Steve buys me pretty socks. They're a deep magenta pink and remind me of an abstract painting. They are perfect. I must be crying a lot. Tears of joy to be alive. Tears of grief to feel such loss. Tears of frustration to be pinned like a butterfly to this bed, numb from the chest down. He's here, he's gone. I'm out of my mind.

Steve says we've been waiting all day to get my new room. And now I'm motion sick from hurtling through space as my hospital bed wheels past rooms and nurses stations. I feel the breeze on my face and I have to close my eyes like windows down on a car ride.

I'm hallucinating from the opiates.

Only I don't know it yet.

I was told I'd be upright and encouraged to practice walking by day two, with permission to bear weight on my leg. But now, I'm told I'm getting a new bed, special for mandatory bed rest and I'm not allowed to be elevated more than a thirty degree angle.

I close my eyes and sleep.

I must not get out of bed for five days. I don't know what's changed. I'm confused as I hear words and explanations and medications and I wonder if this is how my mother felt as she lost her mind to dementia. Just go along willingly, nodding and smiling as the world gets more and more confusing.

I'm getting a new room.

One with a window because I can't stop crying.

And Steve thinks I need to see the trees and sky.

Remember the orderly with the dark teal scrubs and how his eyes matched the color of his shirt? And in my relief of simply being alive with two numb legs and meds coursing through my body, pumping this heart that feels an intense love for everything, immensely grateful for the air we breathe, the beauty of being broken and for the inner workings of a hospital with all these healers who have magic hands to slice through skin and bone.

Jesus, they've seen the inside of me, bone and tumor and muscle and nerve. What must that be like? To re-organize a persons body for them; to cut away death, repair them with bone screws, and sew them together with pigskin.

Remember the orderly with the dark teal scrubs and the eyes to match the color of the deep sea? In my drug-induced state I tell him so.

"Ocean eyes," I say.

"Your eyes match your shirt."

I watch him sweat from his work, positioned at the foot of my bed, in the heat of late August. He stumbled on his words, surprised when I spoke to him. I could see into his past at the little boy he was, just like our own boys in need of kindness and reassurance.

I'm numb from my chest down, I have bruising from my wrists to my elbows from the IVs, I marvel at this concept and the surreal conversation in this place I never expected to be, and being able to see the child inside the young man.

I drop F-bombs when they have to transfer me from one bed to another, the bed sheet a make shift sling,

I am a baby being cradled. I go from love to hate, pain to bliss and back again. But god damn, this special self-inflating bedrest mattress is so comfortable, it's like floating on a sea of deep teal water to match those scrubs and I might never forget the softness in the truth that spills from the vulnerability of being seen.

Chapter Nineteen

There's stability here, in my room full of flowers. The nurses tell me it's their favorite room in the wing because it's quiet and smells like a florist. "You're the only room on this entire floor that doesn't watch TV." They tell me.

Sights and sounds of TV would feel like a sledgehammer to my brain. I want nothing but a peaceful meadow.

"The drugs are entertaining enough." I reply.

It's only after three days that we figure out I've been hallucinating. Yes, the sparkly orbs of light flying around the room like pixies and fairies dancing for my entertainment. Yes, the surrealism of Dali and hospital clocks dripping from concrete walls. IV poles and other furniture melting and disappearing into the floor. Yes, to the voices I perceived as "the muse" instructing me to reach for my phone and type out incoherent texts and page after page of bad prose.

It was only when I woke in the dark to a friendly face in my room, when things went awry. She was carrying a stack of pillows and blankets, teetering on the verge of overflow. *Can you press that help button for me?* She asked nicely, and so I pushed that red button because I didn't want her stack of supplies to spill all over my room. The night nurse arrived asking what it was that I needed.

"I don't know," I shrug,

"She asked me to press the button." I say.

He glanced around the empty room.

"Who asked you?" He says.

I look around the empty room hoping to see the person who had just been standing beside my bed. I shrugged again, there are so many people coming and going here.

"There was a nurse here." I explain.

"With the stack of pillows and blankets."

He's silent, processing the situation.

"She asked me to press the red button for her." I say.

He left the room in a hurry.

My pain management team was called.

And so began the pharmaceutical dance of trial and error. Narcotics. Opiates. Pills to manage the pain but allow me my sanity without hallucinations. Pills to aid sleep. Pills to numb me physically but not depress me into a puddle of sobbing tears. Pills to provide relief that wouldn't simultaneously make me violent towards myself in my bedrest. (I fight demons in my sleep, while being chased by bad guys who wrap arms around me tightly, I wake to the wind being knocked out of me. Come to find out I've punched my self in my own stomach: stitches, tubes, drains and all.)

I have a lack of control and depth perception.

Apparently I am very sensitive to narcotics.

Days later they comment, *You're a medical mystery*. As the nurse runs ice cubes along my leg, charting nerves and pain, they jokingly refer to my zebra stripes of sensation and nerve damage. I am camouflaged on the Serengeti.

I am strolling through gardens, pain free in my dreams.
I am bobbing alone in uncharted territory.
My hospital bed, an inflatable raft.
It's the ship that keeps me afloat.

Steve brushes my teeth.
Steve brushes my hair.
Dizzy dizzy dizzy.

Chapter Twenty

It's day five of bedrest and they are beginning to wean me off the morphine and fentanyl drip. First, weaning me off the epidural that renders me useless from the waist down.

My IV's will be removed tomorrow and I'll practice walking for the first time. The pills come scheduled, on time, delivered in shifts to stay ahead of the pain. The pain is so intense, I wake up to bright lights, thinking I'm in the middle of the highway after being run over by a truck.

I impress my nurse with my breathing exercises: here, suck on this tube to exercise your lungs after surgery and it feels like college bong hits; I'm high on life.

Two occupational therapists visit me with tools I will need to maintain a sense of independence once I leave the hospital. One tool is a long blue strap that loops over my foot so I can manually move my leg towards the edge of the bed. Another tool is a long handled grabber for items dropped on the floor, since I cannot yet stand or even think about bending over. There's a plastic contraption that will put my socks on for me, with the help of ropes I hold and navigate from my reclined position. And then they park my walker in the corner of the room. They let me know a physical therapist will be working with me once I've been given permission to sit up in bed. Once I've been given permission to stand and learn to walk again, I will require both a walker and a wheelchair for an undetermined amount of time.

On Day six, I finally realize how strong my upper body is. Without help, I'm able to log roll myself from a flat bed to seated position although I still require someone to lift my legs for me. My catheter is removed by a nurse in training, they get my permission because it's her first time doing the procedure.

The portable toilet they call a "commode" is parked two feet from my bed. I pee for the first on it and the nurse cheers like I'm a two year old in potty training. She asks if I need her to wipe me.

"No, thank you." I say.

She stares at me because she thinks I look faint.

"So, you're a writer?" she asks.

"Oh, I should give you some privacy."

She realizes my silence, then pulls the curtain.

I'm a fall risk, so they all hover.

After six days I'm allowed to sit up, with the bed finally raised to a 30 degree angle. Today I have to practice standing, I have to bear weight on my leg, and eventually take a few steps with the walker. The physical therapist and Steve help lift me under my arms so I can stand with the walker. I shift weight on both legs, try a baby step with the walker, then back up and sit down again. It's nearly impossible.

I hear my Mom say *Baby steps, Meredith.* And after a moment, they lift me again by my armpits until I am balanced and standing. I'm lightheaded and pale. I proceed to take three steps, turn the walker and sit down into the recliner. I feel accomplished and exhausted and immediately burst into tears.

The smells that rise from my body when I stand and walk for the first time overwhelm me, making me lightheaded. This whole walker situation: two people assisting me by my armpits? It reminds me so much of my Dad that it makes me extremely sad. Taking three steps drained all of my energy. Three fucking steps.

"You have to be able to walk before you can go home." She scolds, and I simultaneously feel like a small child and a crazy woman. I'm a prisoner in my own body.

I already don't like this physical therapist. I hate her, in fact. I hate everything about her. The energy she brings into my room is jarring. She says she won't discharge me. She says I'll have to go to a rehabilitation facility and won't be released to our home. She says I'll need a wheelchair and so Steve starts mentally planning a handicap access ramp design for our front steps. I feel broken and angry and yet she only smiles, reminding me that being there for the first day of Sixth Grade isn't actually that important.

"Focus on the big picture," She lectures.

"You'll be there for his college graduation and wedding."

Who the fuck is this lady? I despise her.

Does she know I had cancer and am only able to look ahead five days, five weeks, five years at a time? I'm so angry at her. It's only after she leaves that I can breathe. From the recliner by the window I watch the trees for about two hours.

A young nurse with wavy brown hair knocks on my door when I call for supervision to get back in bed. Her name is Maggie, like my old sweet dog that died when I was nine months pregnant. Maggie is so kind and familiar and encouraging that I'm able to get out of the recliner on my own and use the walker to walk ten steps to the wall where the physical therapist has put the portable toilet.

Maggie goes about her business while I sit down to pee. I stand up from the toilet all by myself, leaning hard on the walker for support, and then I shuffle in slippers with the walker over to the left side of my bed.

I sit down, and using the blue foot strap my occupational therapist taught me to use, I pull my leg up onto the bed and pull up the sheet to get comfy. Maggie smiles at me so genuinely that I want to hug her. This is the furthest I have walked and I didn't feel lightheaded.

She makes notes in my chart:
Walked unassisted across the length of the room.
She says I'll be discharged to home, possibly tomorrow.

This is the first taste of hope I've had in a week.
There are so many tiny steps required for independence.
I can't believe I used to take walking for granted.

Chapter Twenty-one

You were with me here Dad, but I didn't know it until the day I left my room after five days of bedrest. Six days after surgery, I wheeled myself in a wheelchair and battled lightheadedness while I was encouraged to make a single loop around the hospital wing.

I turned the corner and there you were, we were, both back in rehab with you and your traumatic brain injury and me having just run through the Philly airport to catch a flight. My shoes had caused me blisters that day, but today I wear slippers and a Johnny that opens in the back and a head full of greasy unkempt hair.

You are there waiting for me at the next turn, in the bright blue eyes of my pain management nurse, she looks at me and I see your eyes, and I burst into tears.

It's all so close to grief. All of this. And I find myself having to explain that I'm not in pain, yes I am in pain, but I'm also actually grieving. Every nurse and doctor at Dartmouth knows this story. My walker reminds me of you. The nurses remind me of you too, in how they lift me from under my armpits until I am balanced enough to hold myself up. Just as they lifted you, a 78 year old man, they lift me, a 41 year old woman as I practice walking.

There you are in the middle of the night when the head nurse comes around with pain meds in teeny tiny paper cups and I see you turn to me as you did just a month ago and say in a hushed whisper, *It gets to the point where you just take the pills, Meredith. But I always count them!* Your words echo in my brain before I toss my pills back with a swig of lukewarm water. Every action, a prayer.

Surgery and cancer free.

But still, in that space with your desire to go back home, your frustration is my frustration with a body that cannot perform the way it used to. I stood for that moment in your shoes, in my slippers, and I cried because I get to go home now, but you never did.

I dream this night that I am just strolling around a garden, looking at things. It was so pleasant. I'm pain free in my dreams. I thought I knew what pain was. I had no idea how much pain (and humility) the human body can endure.

I take a shower for the first time in over a week with the help of a kind nurse and a shower seat. It takes all my energy to cross the threshold into the bathroom, where I realize

I can't use a real toilet because my knee and leg muscles won't allow me to be in a seated position. She brings over the portable commode, which has an extra tall seat, and I pee while she turns on the water.

She gets the shower ready and tapes plastic over my drains and tubes to keep them dry. I am completely naked and vulnerable, relying on the kindness of strangers. She washes my body while I sit on the tall shower seat, holding onto my walker. She's much shorter than me and certainly getting wet while she reaches out to wash my hair. I'm so greasy, I feel like a seal.

"We'll get you all spiffy," she says, and it makes me miss my mom. Steve will be here any minute and the nurses will teach him how to give me the required shot in my stomach, because I'm unable to stick a needle in my own body. He'll administer this shot at the same time every day for the next four weeks. As soon as he learns how, we'll be free to go home. Today is my seventh day post surgery.

Home is three hours away, and we drive across the lawn to get as close to the front steps as possible. Steve and my 72 year old father-in-law carry me, in my wheelchair, up our stairs and into our house.

I am home.

Part III

Chapter Twenty-two

March 2017

My mother taught me many things, and today the reminder is to carry on. *Onward and upward*, as she would say. Through dark and light, life is a beautiful mess of the two. But always always, go towards love.

Our plane lands in heat and humidity. I have a wedding dress packed in my suitcase and our three boys have khaki shorts and blue button up shirts packed in theirs. We are eloping, and it's the first time all five of us are on a plane together. Unbelievable really, the place life takes you.

After landing in St. Thomas, we locate our rental Jeep and make our way to the Airbnb apartment. Steve drives and I cringe each time a car passes, disoriented with driving on the wrong side of the road, everything feels new and unexplored and makes me feel strangely alive.

Two flights up and our balcony overlooks the ocean. We figure out who will be sleeping where, and then we pause to take in the view. We've been here all of twenty minutes when my phone rings.

While the boys bicker over if they will snorkel or swim in the pool, I hear my mother's hospice nurse through the static. "She's dying, Meredith. It won't be long." She says.

I am speechless. She keeps talking to me, with explanations, heart rates, oxygen levels, color of skin; my mouth goes dry and I sit down hard on the bed. "I literally just landed here in St. Thomas. I'm supposed to get married in three days. What am I supposed to do?"

Now it's her turn for silence. She has no answers for me, no motherly advice that will rid me of guilt or blame or grief or confusion. There is no right answer.

She's peaceful they say.

They say not to come.

The nurse suggests I speak to my mother and tell her all the things I need to say, just in case. She tells me she'll call me back in twenty minutes, and during that time I text a circle of close friends, asking for advice.

Do I leave? Do I book a flight for Virginia and miss my own wedding? What the fuck am I supposed to do?

Where you are right now is the place you are supposed to be. My mother's best friend tells me this in all caps and a bold face font, a reminder of what my mom would tell me herself if she could. By the time my phone rings again, I have decided that my mother would want me to stay. She would want me to get married.

I don't know if this is right or wrong.

I don't know anything anymore.

The hospice nurse calls me and holds her phone up to my mother's ear so she can hear my voice, and I tell her everything in my heart.

She's there, she's here.

She's everywhere with me, always.

I'm standing with my feet on sand, two of our boys splashing in the pool behind me. What do you say that might be the last thing you say to your mother before she dies? *I love you I love you I love you.*

I begin a stream of consciousness, picturing her curled in her hospital bed, mouth agape. I speak to her as if I were sitting next to her, I'm standing at the beach, Mom, your favorite place in the world and the waves are lapping my feet. You taught me this. My love for the ocean is your love for the ocean, Mom.

I continue on with memories of us floating in Maine, in New Jersey, in Virginia. I talk and talk until my throat is sore. I talk through tears. I'm getting married, Mom, and your spirit will be here with us. I know this. I'm going to get married here and then I'll get on a plane for Virginia. But if you want to go be with Dad before I can get there, then I want you to be free. It's the most beautiful place I've ever seen, Mom. You would love it here. Your friends tell me you would want me to be here and get married. But I'll get to you as soon as I can, I promise. It's hard to catch my breath but I force the words out anyway, possibly the last thing I say.

(And the most important)

Thank you for being my Mom.

Chapter Twenty-three

Patent leather Maryjane's with ruffled socks. Tea and coffee cake after church, the high-heeled shoes of women clicking across the tile floor. Looking for God in the stained glass windows of an old stone sanctuary.

Once again I'm crying in the Portland airport, one gate over from where I sat last July when my father died.

I choose my seat wisely because I have my mother's superstitions in me and I don't want to recreate what happened when I missed my father's death by just a few hours.

Hey Mom, It's the first of March. The sun is shining in Maine, and snowflakes are swirling and I feel strangely at peace with your death. No one can believe you held on for these seven days until I was able to fly to Virginia. But I'm coming now, to sit with you and hold your hand, to sing to you and read to you as you take your last breath on Earth.

You had a beautiful life, you taught me strength and it's how I keep moving forward now. And I will somehow continue to move forward without you. But how do I walk towards the thing that scares me most?

Chapter Twenty-four

There are blossoms on the trees here. Even as death is happening, it's strange to think that life is happening too. I'd be lying if I said I wasn't scared. But I'm here. Sometimes the hardest thing, like sitting with your mother as her spirit leaves her body, begins with just one step. I am one of three children and yet I'm the only one here.

A night nurse brings in a huge platter of food "for the family" and finds only me. It depresses me and I have no appetite anyway; so I let it sit there on my mother's dresser, untouched, until the staff shift changes.

Another nurse, more familiar with our family situation, finds me asleep in a straight chair, bent at the waist, with my head on my mother's bed. She wakes me, and hugs me, and immediately locates me a sleeping recliner from the common area, dragging it into the small room. She has known my family for years, and she knows I will not be leaving this room until my mother dies.

She also knows I will be the only one of her children to be present here. She retrieves the platter, apologizing as she hands me a plate of scrambled eggs the kitchen made for me this morning.

My heart knows all too well that parental illness has the power to fracture and dissolve family, as it did when my mom was diagnosed. Seeing and experiencing that tragedy was double the loss: fathers and brothers vanishing from the peripheral. Without a mother we are a family of orphans.

A former military family, what we experienced was the silo syndrome, and it's the catastrophe of coping mechanisms. We can't be too hard on ourselves, it's just how it all played out, unfortunately. But I know that my mother would be heartbroken to know how we handled her illness.

This isolating, finger-pointing, melancholic thread weaves itself through our life. Sewing us together in a way that divides and joins like nothing else, like nothing I asked for, yet all that was given, and all that remains.

So, how do I do this? I wonder.

Just take one step.

One bite of egg at a time.

It's life and death, weddings and funerals.

Hers was a beautiful life.

And I'm here to witness its end.

Chapter Twenty-five

My mother lost her own mother at age nineteen. She always told me I reminded her of her mom, not my tall stature because her own mother was very petite - but I suppose it was her spirit and free will. *Barefoot and bra-less* was how Mom described her, shaking her head at the memory of her 1950's mother, marching to the beat of her own drum.

I think of this as I caress my mom's hair and hold her hand as she begins struggling for breath. Each intake gets harder, each pause between breaths stretches into forever.

I watch this process repeat for hours upon hours and think of her and her mother, and their own complicated dynamic through life and death. By the time my mother was twenty-five she had lost both of her parents.

I'm sitting on the edge of my chair, the recliner I have

slept in for five nights, with her hand in mine. I barely sleep, unable to take my eyes off her. Unable to let go of her hand and this last connection in the physical world.

I've been here for five nights, with my face as close as possible to hers. I describe to her how it would feel to walk with bare feet on the sand, to feel the ocean waves when her feet have not felt the earth in years. There is no end, I tell her, there's only the tide that comes and goes.

Each breath grows more raspy and each exhale becomes an audible sigh. It's through these sighs that she allows me to hear her voice after being mute for years. It is beautifully heartbreaking, the sound of her voice, so tender and innocent.

She has never looked more childlike to me. She must be scared or anxious on some subconscious level I suppose, as she ventures into this unknown. She never wavers though, she never shows it but still I remind her not to be scared.

"I'll be with you the whole time until you're ready."

"We'll find each other again, maybe in the next life."

"You'll be free from pain and suffering."

I tell her things that I truly believe.

Chapter Twenty-six

Her breathing is shallow and rhythmic like an underwater current that moves you while snorkeling, the slightest hint of seasickness in my heart and stomach. I watch her chest rise and fall. There is an overwhelming sense of calm.

We sleep holding hands, tethered to each other. I am her buoy until she's ready to let go. It's been a ninety-six hour vigil and sunrise will greet us soon. She's such a strong and brave fighter and is holding on, as if she's waiting for something.

Her journey to death feels excruciatingly slow and yet every last minute is a gift. The strength of her heart thumping away is a tribute to her strong spirit. Her nurses and I had no idea that she would make it through that first night, that second morning, that third sunset.

Days blur together in a series of shift changes. Nurses and friends: stories, tears, and laughter. This room is the holiest of churches I've yet prayed in. Sitting next to my mothers dying body with the blinds open as the sun rises pink and blue across the sky, there is nothing but love.

"Rise and shine!" She would say each morning.

I'm sitting in the same nursing home, the same room where my father died. My mother lays dying next to the same window that was opened to release my father's spirit.

I hold my mother's hand and sing in my off-key voice, the one I inherited from her. My father died while I was on my way to be with him. And yet when I arrived and his body lay prone, he looked nothing like himself, nothing like my father. And I was surprised by the force field around his bed that kept me at a distance and eventually brought me to tears.

Is this the difference of mothers and fathers? Is this why I can hold and touch, and lay my head on my mother's body? Perhaps because she grew me, birthed me, raised me in his absence? These thoughts swirl around me.

She is Sleeping Beauty, at peace for the first time in the body that no longer serves her. "It's okay to let go," I tell her. "Be free and find me again." I squeeze her hand, picturing a little girl skipping down the coast of Maine, as she once was, hauling a pot of saltwater for the lobster boil.

I tell her my secrets.
I tell her my fears.
Her eyes remain closed.

Chapter Twenty-seven

Each evening my best friend from high school stops by with dinner. She and I used to get drunk from my mother's boxed wine during our teenage rebellion and now she shows up in a power suit and heels, fresh from the court room.

We share stories and memories of marching band, first boyfriends, and teenage angst from lifetimes ago. We sit together, watching my mother's chest rise and fall. She hugs me before leaving, each night we think it's my mother's last.

Each day my mother's best friend Sue stops by to join me in my mothers room. I sit with my feet up in the recliner, hoping to prevent swelling in my hip and leg. She and I have never spent this much time together, and it's a real gift. We talk about everything, while my mother lays beside us. It was my mother who brought us together, this way, and it makes us both smile to think how much she would have loved joining in this conversation. And I believe that she was, in her own way, joining in this conversation, a circle of women sharing stories, a ceremony being held at her death bed.

I only leave the room if Sue is present to sit with my mom. My fear of abandonment is a role reversal and I don't want my mother to experience my absence. I take my cane and walk to the bathroom and back. Sometimes it's breakfast, or lunch or dinner and other dementia residents are in the dining room awaiting a meal that they often insist on paying for. The nurses play along, acting as servers who happen to wear scrubs in this restaurant found in this demented world, where purses are left without wallets or cash to pay for meals; and they tell these residents who fret with agitation, "The bill has been taken care of! Enjoy your evening."

There's a trio of ladies that everyone calls The Golden Girls. They walk and chat and believe themselves to be out in the world and not trapped behind locked doors in this beautiful memory center created specifically for dementia. It is the most strange and beautiful and sad arrangement of friendship I have ever witnessed.

Dementia will do this to a person, it cracks open the skull and rearranges reality. People get locked in loops of cleaning and rearranging furniture, of worry for the adult child gone missing. People get agitated over the bank being closed or the need for sweaters and coats.

On this night when I leave my mother's room, as I have done for five days, I walk past The Golden Girls waiting for their meal to be served. I've seen them here for months, if not years, and I know their dynamic. I know their backstory and know how the nurses speak to them to calm them, or ask them to lead the activities, since they are the three most cognitively advanced residents in this particular wing.

On my walk to the bathroom, I smile and say hello to them, and only two of them smile back at me. Upon returning to my mother's room, I pass the dining room again, walking slowly with my cane.

I hear the louder most outspoken Golden Girl speak:

"There she goes again! There's the new girl."

And I look up to see all of their eyes upon me.

They believe that I am their peer, that they are my age, not the age of my mother. They believe I'm a resident here, in this strange community they've landed in (and never think to question). They believe I'm the *new girl* with the cane who rudely never joins them and instead takes her meals in the privacy of her room.

I close the door behind me and sit down to tell this story to Sue, intermittently laughing and crying as I do. I can't help but think of how much pleasure my father would have had in knowing this: that The Golden Girls thought I actually lived here. He would've found it so incredibly funny.

Chapter Twenty-eight

I can do this. I can't do this.

Frustration, peace, anger, boredom, sadness, fatigue, discomfort (both physical and emotional) and still I sit here; just as I know she would have done for me. If she had been able, she would have never left my bedside seven months ago after my cancer surgery, I know this to be true.

Sitting vigil at my mother's bedside is the strangest form of meditation I've ever known. Singing, reading aloud, and listening to her favorite songs. I work through each and every emotion possible while seated next to her.

The uncertainty of not knowing what this will look like is what slays me. Will it be dark outside when she dies? Will I know her last intake? Will I hear her last exhale? Will it be peaceful or will it leave me with an unpleasant sound I won't be able to erase from my mind? Will she allow me to be present or will she wait until I step out for more water or a bathroom break?

Her breath is so shallow, her lips so pale and cold. I feel as though I am a new mother again, watching my infant sleep. I'm once again watching and learning and finding my way. The complicated mix of emotions that come with the birth-life-death cycle, it's happening before my very eyes and I feel like a bad actress in a shitty movie that I don't want to watch. I've never done anything like this and it's not something that will ever be repeated.

I keep asking my dad, "Where are you?"

He died in this same room.

Two-hundred and thirty days ago.

"Are you coming to meet her?"

"Can you take her hand as she lets go of mine?"

I talk to spirits. I talk to ghosts.

I talk to the walls that contain our hearts.

Chapter Twenty-nine

I can almost feel the beloved corduroy couch of my childhood. The one that we all napped upon. Drool and dreams, and awakening to wide whale corduroy imprints across our sleepy faces.

Reality becomes distorted at the 3am hour with the administering of pain meds and repositioning of her fragile body and wound care for bedsores that I can't bear to look at, I'm so thankful for her nurses.

I dim the lights and tuck her in. Her twitching increases and everything seems wrong. It's all wrong and this really fucking sucks and I'm scared and she's looking more like a skeleton than my mother and that's when the fear takes over.

I'm so very tired. What if she dies while my eyes are closed? What if I wake to find that I'm holding her hand and it's cold and she's dead? I lean my head back, I keep hold of her hand and close my eyes anyway. Waking an hour later, her breathing continues but the light in the room has changed and feels more like peace.

Her hospice nurse asked again, hoping my oldest brother would agree to talk to my mom so she could just hear his voice. The dying process is painful and my mom is holding on too long, she says. My mother has been on hospice for two and a half years, her hospice care manager knows the inner workings of our dysfunctional family. She explains gently that maybe my mom needs permission from all of her children. Maybe she needs to hear at least one of my brothers voices after years of silence. So we text, it's a delicate dance of the estranged. He agrees to speak to her and then I dial his phone number.

"Hi, I'm here with Mom." I say.

"I'm going to put you on speakerphone now."

He replies with clearly enunciated words.

I feel as though we are reading from a script.

The harsh words spoken over years float between us.

Our mother is in a semi comatose state with one eye open, one eye closed. But she registers voices; every one of her nurses reminds me that hearing is amplified at death. And she moves her eye and blinks while she listens to him describe the snowstorm around him in Colorado on the mountain. He shares the memories of her zipping him up

95

in his snowsuit as a child in Chicago and New Jersey. His words flow for nearly ten minutes and my tears fall on her pillow while I hold the phone next to her ear.

I feel at peace knowing we've attempted to build this bridge, that we've done everything we can think of to give her permission to now let go of life and end her suffering. I'm proud of him too, for being brave enough to speak his heart to her. Her illness tore our family apart but there's hope that her death may bring us together. I sleep holding her hand, surprised to find her still alive in the morning.

Chapter Thirty

By mid-day there's an energetic quickening and the nurses seem to know they need to say goodbye.

At the 3pm shift change, staff comes in one by one to hug me and stroke my mother's head. I can't break my gaze with her, I cannot leave the room to provide them any privacy. I cannot move from this chair. When dinnertime rolls around, they insist that I eat but I'm not hungry.

At 11pm the shift changes once again and more nurses knock gently on the door. They stand with tears in their eyes, looking at my mother. How many times have they seen death? How many goodbyes have they given?

I hold my mother's hand as nurses tell me story after story, the early years of my mother's diagnosis and the later years. We laugh together and we cry together.

My mother has lived here longer than any resident, and they have all cared for her deeply. When the room quiets again after midnight, it's just the two of us holding hands.

In the dark of night, I open the window.
The Spring air smells of Magnolia blooms.
Gracefully, peacefully; as she lived, she died.

Chapter Thirty-one

How is it possible that in her death she looked most like her youthful self? There was such peace in her face in those last days and hours. When the pain succumbed to morphine and her muscles relaxed with a letting go, it was like saying goodbye to my real and true mother, not the mask of dementia that had robbed her from us for the previous seven years. Witnessing her strength and peaceful death had a profound effect, and for that I will always be grateful. Watching the love that rose up and completely surrounded her in her final hours was a testament to how she lived her days. She was the strongest woman I have ever known.

The day before my mother died, I told her of the sunset I saw that glowed orange. After six days of filth, when Mom's best friend, Sue, told me I had to go shower at her house.

She insisted, and reminded me that she would sit with my mom and call me immediately if there were any sudden changes. In her spritely small stature, born the same week as my mother, the same year, in the same New England state. She tells me this matter-of-factly:

"As your honorary mother..."

"I'm saying this because I love you."

"You need to bathe yourself and wash your hair."

Sue's house was literally two minutes away, in the same neighborhood where I attended Junior High. I made that familiar drive and climbed into her shower and cried.

Before my mom died, I told her of the sunset I saw when I left Sue's house that evening, the glowing orange sky and the Great White Heron that flew over my car, reflecting the peach light on its belly and wings.

Before she died, I told my mom that it gave me peace and also reminded me of her, that I've always seen her in the freedom of birds in flight.

Now, just four hours after she took her last breath, I'm in the car driving that same stretch of road that divides the wetlands and the marsh. And there's the Great White Heron, flying the same path, this time in the morning light of sunrise. Sailing with its wide wings over my car once again.

"Hi mom." I say aloud, "I love you."

Chapter Thirty-two

I had told her we would be okay. And the truth is, we will be okay. A week from today my father's ashes will find their final resting place at the nation's cemetery with full military honors and a 21 gun salute.

The day after his funeral, we'll be celebrating my mother at her memorial service. Her ashes will be surrounded by flowers and friends and photos of her amazing life.

This week I'm wrapping my head around writing her obituary. After all these years and a lifetime of love and loss between this day and the next, I can quote all the details and all the years of teaching and service, the lives she touched and the joy she shared, but what matters most?

She was loved she was loved she was loved.

Epilogue

No one truly knows how to do grief. It tosses you in a cesspool and you muck about in the shit. You pray that grief and bitterness does not become you, while the rest of the world carries on.

Sadness ebbs and flows with anger, and a rage that burns like fire until exhausted. This repeats over and again, for months and years, possibly; until some random day much later, the last fire to consume you finally smolders and loses its power over you. And there's no celebration, just a deep exhale like a weight has been lifted from your chest. And you don't even know what to do with yourself because it's been such a long tiring road.

So you just keep walking towards what buoys you, each step a prayer, *yes please, and thank you.*

Meredith Winn is a self taught, imperfect human who takes joy in the simple pleasure of being alive. In her past life she worked as a teacher, seamstress, photographer, freelance writer, magazine editor, printmaker and textile designer.

She studied forestry in college in the early 90's and ran a solar installation company for a decade into the early 2000's. Meredith was born on the West coast, spent her childhood on the East coast, lived as a young adult in the Rocky Mountains and became a mother in the American South. She relocated to New England from Austin, Texas in 2011. Meredith is a bone cancer survivor and a year-round ocean swimmer. She and her husband raised their blended family in an off-grid yurt nestled in the mountains and now live by the tides, on an island three miles out to sea, off the coast of Maine.

@MeredithWinnStudio
www.meredithwinn.com

www.ingramcontent.com/pod-product-compliance
Lightning Source LLC
Chambersburg PA
CBHW020744130626
46554CB00006B/2136